The Cloud Effect

Rodney Cloud Hill

The Cloud Effect © 2016 Rodney Cloud Hill (@HiphopIngenuity)

Illustrations by: Brandon Wright (@Bdavonthaartist)
& Weston Parmelee (@Westonparmelee)

Photography by: Santanna Hayes (@Santannaphotog)
Co-Poet in "Stand": Nigel Scott (@VaThePoet)

ISBN-13: 978-1535426879
ISBN-10: 153542687X

Printed in the United States of America
All Rights Reserved. No part of this book may be reproduced or transmitted in any form or by any means, without the express permission in writing from the author and/or publishing company.

Author Contact: clouddanceking@yahoo.com
Prysmatic Dreams Publishing

www.PrysmaticDreamsPublishing.info

This book is dedicated to The Creator,

all of those in society and this magnificent thing we call life.

Contents

The Initiation 1

God's Plan for a Shaded Revolution 3

Unlearn 6

Letter to Abel Tesfaye AKA (The Weeknd) 8

Find You First 11

Beautiful Deception 13

Stand 16

Negative Immune System 19

How to Tame a Sinner 22

A Letter to the Jump Offs 24

Complacence 27

Struggling Hearts 30

Religious Ball Game 32

The Verdict 35

Are You an OG 38

Casket Coated Mindset 41

The Contract 43

The Final Rest 45

Death's Wish 47

The Rehearsal 49

When Will We 51

Mothers Reflection 53

The Closure 55

The Initiation

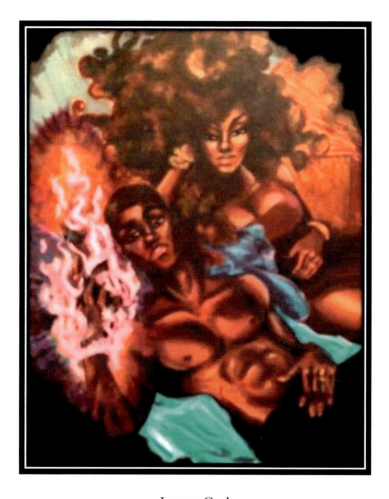

I am a God
Yes, no really
I am a God
Trapped in a box
Plagued to be inadequate
You are my kingdom
I have seen the potential in your eyes long before your thoughts
became diluted

and since I realized mine I have learned more than any college professor could teach me
on a chalk board
I have written out my future long before my birth
Destined to bless stages and inspire nations.
I wonder
I'm speaking to you
What did you want to be before your creativity died
I pray that I can bring beauty from ink
Let my pen prosper between the cheeks of your margins
Seek difference and glory with every stroke
Be my garden and blossom my endeavors into existence
Take me
Take me to a place far from here
So on this stage
It removes your flaws
You my listeners, are the proof of heavens existence within minutes
You are my crowd
My guidance
I need you just as much as you need my verbal pleasures
You are my golden gates of life
I will bless you until death due us part
I am the poetic disciple and you are my muse
You give me meaning
My reason to love
My reason to strive
My reason to live
My reason to
Thank you

God's Plan for a Shaded Revolution

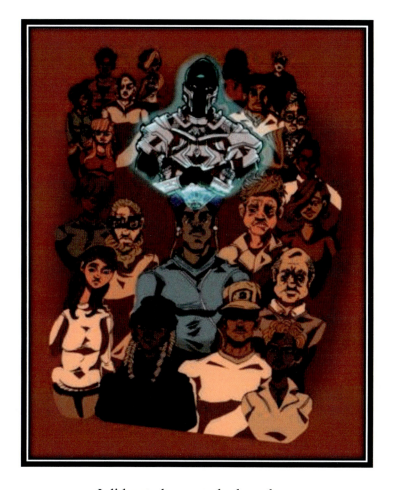

I did not choose to be born here
My ancestral lineage died with every agonizing step taken toward a slave ship named Jesus
Save me
Save us was all you heard
From mothers men and children
In my native tongue
A language that I can no longer speak of
Because I was forced to give up my true heritage
Beaten until I was lifeless
It only makes sense that the decisions for my soul became someone

else's
The day my people stepped foot in America
Sold my melanin that was supposed to be priceless on auction blocks
Are you mixed
Oh you must be adopted
That's what I heard all my life
Why are your parents dark skinned and you are beige
Why do you even speak up for the struggle
You can't be a true brother
You are a house nigga
Nigga
The tone of my body skipped generations to give me a chance in white America
A chance that from which I did not ask for
Funny thing is I haven't been treated equally by them since birth
and by some of my own race i'm looked upon as a curse
But I am presently trying to free the minds of thousands
While you discuss the hate of my physical features
Nigga
I did not choose my complexion
My great grandmother was forced to bare children from a man of European descent
FORCED
So you can miss me with the mouth of Willie Lynch's tongue
A plan that is going all so well when quote unquote real niggas and real bitches abide by it
Spoken from transparent outlines of a human beings
Do you not know anything of your history
I can't fully blame you
When you have taken in everything of western society as if it was your own
You let the man become your savior awhile ago
They killed off all our true leaders and replaced them with black friendly faces
As we continue to sweep it under the rug
But it's All apart God's plan they say
Really nigga
No action is God's plan

That's slave mentality at its finest and complacency is how they gain checkmate
We could overtake them with our pawns
Is it the fear of death that frightens you
Because that is coming far sooner than you think
Martial law is a door step away
I just find it sad that
I see the potential of your so called lord in every one of you
You just have to see him in yourself today

Unlearn

In school we were taught that negroes have no history
As if our lives started on the plantation fields
and by the looks of things
In the year 3000
We will be nothing more than Love & HipHop, Kanye West, and BET memories
I'm not a prophet but the words I speak are prophetic
and these coons make it damn easy to see the future
One of man's worst problems is
We actually believe our life is more important than the next
A stepping stool of deceit
We put celebrities on a pedestal
Forget that Gods and Goddesses ever existed
and that their blood flows through our veins
Not just chosen few
But today
Today, everything has the taste of manipulation
Elementary has become a prison with jungle gyms
Psychiatrist diagnosing our children with any symptom they can find
Medicating the mentality of geniuses
For the prevention of thinking outside the box

and by high school you are brainwashed to follow this
Capitalistic society
Known as democracy
Be and do as the men before you
and by graduation you might dodge a casket quick
Quit
As if they don't already think a body bag is all a black man is good for
What our ancestors stood for
Died for
It can't be this
They say the struggle is real
No, no the struggle is the new Israel
Paving the way for slaves to be secluded in the surface
Serpents
Staining the youth to do more than bite the fruit
It's like food for thought for bulimics
Why force feed knowledge when you're just going to throw it up anyway
The old heads said change was going to come
Shit that could be any day
See, see where I'm from
If you make it
They will try to do anything to knock you off your feet
You talking about the white man
Yeah the white man, the white man
Blame it on the white
No, nigga you don't see them killing over pairs of jump mans
Well I have a new balance to get you further
That's a shoe reference for you brothers
Since it's the only thing you seem to get it on time
Fragile minds
Seeking to be freed
Searching for salvation
Without bravery to take the lead
Pawns trying to make it through life to score
You can complain about the struggle
Im going be that chess piece playing off the board

Letter to Abel Tesfaye AKA (The Weeknd)

Tonight
I free myself from these shackles
Minds have been swollen from false teachings composed on my people
For generations
We succeeding in removing the bindings from our ancestor's ankles
but placed them on our heads
Instead of the crowns deserved for all humanity
"We Belong to this World"

Yet we constantly destroy its innocence
We have made every human that looks different from your skin
Color an "Enemy"
So the fact that God put us all on earth for a reason
is "Lost in orbit"
A suicidal constellation brought to you by man
Astrology for the blind
You do not have to be "High for This"
To know it makes sense
Instead cents is placed as the primary option
Leaving so many "Nomad" in self-worth
Distortion
Tell me who's apart of "The Knowing"
Is it you little girl
The one who's adolescent in mind but adult in age
So the only thing in life she strives for
Is to find
The "Rolling Stone" at "The Party"
You crave on your time off
Or is it you little boy?
The one who's turned a woman's shrine
Into a open garden
To be ravaged through from "Crew Love"
I rather spend my time in a "House of Balloons"
Comic strip communications
Thinking caps to capitalize on life's endeavors
Indeed
We live in an era where
Giving jewels has become a mental landslide and kicking knowledge
has been tainted with "Wicked Games"
The moral compasses we once held have been tossed into the
Bermuda Triangle
"Love in the Sky" is disguised by selfish envisioning
Pain is molded and amplified to be our demise
The ambition to do better is now filled with "Loft Music"
An empty space containing negative motivation.
You see, today's focus is pussy and dick
and don't get me wrong I love sex
But I be damn If I let it control my every decision

See, see
I need vagina that can do more than just make me cum
and I could tell by her physical accent it was only going to be
"One of those Nights"
So in "The Morning"
When you kick out your trophy buried within your bedsheets
Do you feel accomplished
or is your room dismayed with "Echoes of Silence"
The sexual violence orchestrated by Satan's violins
Sin, with blurred lens
Realizing
When are we going to do more than just live for "The Weeknd"

Find You First

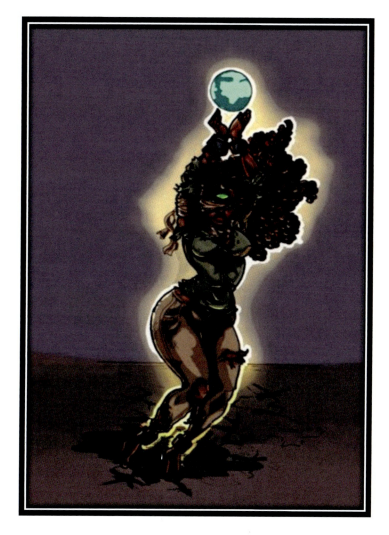

My type
My type is short in dark skin
but not like you more like her
A queen
That will never give into society's out take on a woman
She has the body of a goddess and the mind of a revolution
Her whispers stir up caution signed promises
Mother earth

Please don't settle for anything less than a man
Let me gain entrance into your fortune
and expand in your natural horizon
Let me gaze into your sinless pastures and rebirth my iniquities
You are my faith destined from its original origin
My primordial soup of life
You see
My type's skin needs no cover girl
She has already drunken from the fountain of youth
The only blemishes she holds is that from which her shadow makes
because shadows do no justice to her features
Yet it's a silhouette I would still make love too
Two of us destined to be chest pinned for eternity
This sin holds no regrets
You see I lust for you
and people tend to confuse God's perception with misconception
When it was already written
This love is preordained
and I refuse to let past afflictions degrade your worth
When all the females in my life have felt like illusions rehearsed
Sketches that were left with no artistic integrity
It hurts
But when you enter my life
and that day comes
I will know what do with you
I would get on one knee off of first glance
and use our future for the diamond
A glisten far more than any rock can show
Goals of a man ready to accept commitment
Like Egypt accepted slavery
You will be my royalty
My gift from the Nile
I just have to find you first

Beautiful Deception

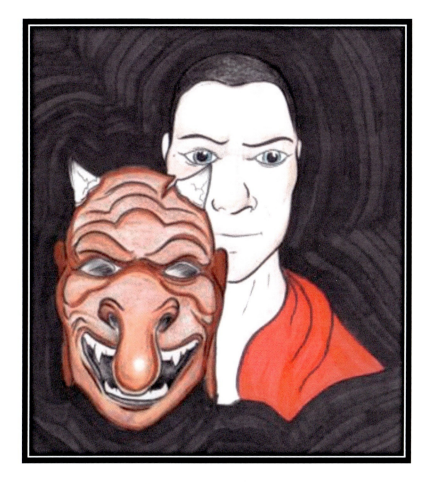

We live in an era where
Love is hated to be committed by commitment
Honesty is restricted
Being real is said often but is resented
Bearing all absence of what's witnessed
and the judge decides the wrong sentence
Who can be a critic.
Someone who's life is livid.
Makes the right wishes but involves gimmicks to keep them vivid
My life should simplistic with these logics but the statistics show different

So I keep watches not to tell time
but to embed in my mind that nothing lasts forever
finally, I get hip
admit my flaws
I have lied the majority of my life to get whatever I wanted
but I use these bars to cement my testimony over the clause
Karma sets in
A liar's diary
Full of blunt imagery sometimes forgotten or is it misplaced to be forgetful
The absence of truth seems inevitable when you refuse to believe in it at first glance
Honestly honesty holds no boundaries because the barricade is shifted
To prevent yourself from being convicted
When the bars aren't even solid to hold confinements
The mouth plays it's own solitary
Anything goes is the game
Goal is to not be judged correctly
With no one to bare witness a silent testimony is slightly achieved
Any advances
No
Conclusion
Your audience is still not deceived
When are you going to learn facts always seep through
when trying to be deceitful
But yet you still continue to lie
Do your lungs ignite when false words roll out
or is your soul empty
When we kiss
Is it the closest your tongue has ever come to the truth
If so I hope karma bites it off so you can never misuse words again
I hope when you think of a false answer God leaves your cerebral bleeding
Is that too harsh
No that's pride talking
Pride
The neglectful ways of unfulfilling an apologetic emotion

Even when you could screw over someone's future in a split second
A surround sound of blindness
I wonder does Sony create vast speakers pulsating with false sounds
Waiting to be dismantled for the truth
Because I know humans do amongst themselves
The art of lies, pathological, sophisticated deception
When God created a voice I know he did not intend for this
To beg someone to believe in a lie without retaining the consequence
of an unjust action.
To argue with your lover
Knowing you just gave your sexual essence to a lucky scavenger
Waiting to watch your relationship go from a rainbow
To a Holocaust being thrown through the sky
Immaturity when you can't use the knowledge instilled in you
By our Creator to rule out right from wrong
We did not buy this
But might as well be CENTS of KNOWLEDGE
because it's common to pay for someone's lack of it
It only seems plausible to expand your earnings to have a
MINDFUL
income

Stand

Stand
In school we were taught that negroes have no history
As if our lives started on the plantations fields
Stand
Brought to the land of the free
With shackles on our feet and locks on our thoughts
Stand
False deliverance embedded in us by our oppressor's teachings
Stand up for the immoral confines traced in brail
Stitched in our ancestors' lashings
I would appreciate if you acknowledge my black skin
Because it seems like sin wasn't in existence until we became your
so called burden
Stand off in the background while mother gives birth
to an off shade child
Tears fill my eyes

As love burns my heart
And anger thrives my temple
Simply, motions reaches it's potential
But little reaction shows face
Attempts to erase the trace of my roots
But this pencil is God's grace
Stand on the DC streets marching with the strongest million man army
I'm far from the words they call me
Thick skin from whip lashes so your words will never insult me
I, stand in the back alley trying to fight off Hitler's German shepherds
Their bites rip my flesh
But their teeth will never penetrate my soul
My heart is gold
I mean my heart is bold
More bold than a bad hand in black jack but This blackjack will never fold
I Stand on my 40 acres and a mule
No
Stand
On the many countries we once ruled
But pulled from royalty to become mentally fooled
Stand
Bring back the original lady of liberty that stands in a white gown with broken shackles at her wrist and feet
A virgin who left the streets running red
but this ain't no menstrual cycle
It's untold knowledge shot by life's missing rifle
No scope
No justice
No hope
How many of us must be sacrificed before the realization kicks in
How many more lynching's before we make amends and end the trend
that we are up against
See it was suicide to put to me up to this
But this speech will allow freedom to be removed from my bucket list

Freedom
I am Martin Luther King turning in my grave because these generations confused my prophetic dream with inceptions limbo
I am Malcolm X standing on this stage brave
Before gunned downed by my own kinfolk
I am Harriet Tubman who once released slaves
but in this day in age psychological nooses keeps our minds in a maze
See I am Marcus Garvey
I am bob Marley
I am the mystery behind Tupac's autopsy
I am Frederick Douglas
I am W E B Dubious
I am Rosa Parks on the bus trying to keep my poise
I am my ancestors
I am the present
I am a man penning hope into the masses
So we all
Can STAND

Negative Immune System

What is fame
Nowadays the talentless gets noticed more than actual rare ability
When's the last time you been fascinated by someone's actions
Yet, you see a million reactions and likes with supporting these ignorant websites
Divide the fractions and pull the wool from over your eyes
I guess that makes them magicians
Illusions conformed to fool the masses and it's working

Are you comfortable
Are you comfortable listening to a song that degrades every female that walks on this earth
As a woman how can you hear the lyrics and bob to that shit
As a man, how were you born
Were you pushed out calling your mother a bitch
Grabbing her tits and forcing her to feed you
No
Well I fear for every child conceived while listening to a so called Chief Keef or Waka Flocka Flame album
Turn up might be the baby's first words
And the sad part is
Some of you would say awwwww
These are the thoughts that consume my mentality while you go through your daily lives
How can I diffuse every negative horizon that's being educated to our youth
Society is looking upside down and the skylines have fallen from its gravitational pull
I have to constantly fight back tears because of the realization of the next generations to come
I fear
I fear life 30 years from now
When you might be able to twerk your way through college
Not on a stripper pole
But academics
Because media is damn sure making it the new fad
So be nostalgic for me
Can you revisit every nutrient consumed as a child
The bittersweet morals taught to you beneath your parents grasp
Some of these kids coming up aren't blessed to say the same and its funny
Not like haha funny
But when you see children clips
Bad ass of the week on Worldstar hiphop
Cursing out their parent
And you have the nerve to repost and endorse it
You don't deserve to be one
Is this where humanity has grown to be

When acts of fame can teach the entire world to reverse its
biological clock
Does anyone care anymore
Are you all going to watch
If so, can you do me a favor
Give me a shell to the head
I don't want fame
I would rather die being the BIG SHOT
Become a martyr
As my blood splatters on the high rises
I know my DNA is worth more
Every droplet scattered will spread my poetry
and Like HIV
I will be known for decomposing this negative immune system

How to Tame a Sinner

I want to know your mind
Don't let time manipulate your thoughts to sin
Idol imagery leaned us towards blasphemous ways in the past
I wonder why if Eve bit the fruit first
Why do men have Adam's apples
Just food for thought mistaken for a lover's lost
Window of opportunity
When the opportunist is a visionary for a passionate distribution of

pleasure
These words unzipped your dress
Long before my fingers made interlude
Your lips moist with vague temptation
Your eyes spoke of deep penetration
Now, now
I have made females cry during sex
but never heard one moan in a conversation
When we were only talking about zodiacs, religion, and politics
I guess this centaur shot his arrow into your inner thighs
That's a Sagittarius reference for the slow ones in the crowd
I be the four legged beast
Ready to please my Nubian queen
Just feed my knowledge
Sapiosexual
See now I have your attention
I will show you how to tame a sinner

A Letter to the Jump Offs

How are you doing Ms
Or would you rather me call you bitch
That's your name in bed right
And all these bitches be like
On sites
Despite the demanding respect from females you recompense no rights
When you refuse to see the moral imbalance in that
What's your passion
I know it has to be more than the 30 minutes of pleasure you obtain every time you dial this number

Do I bring life into you every time I stroke your soul
Are you gaining knowledge when you give me heads up because my passion
My passion, is to spark a revolution into every mind I come across
Even if the decisions you make with me tend to leave you face down
Does biting the pillow bend back the reality
That your body is proportioned
To a thought process that screams this will go nowhere
I never bless your lips with a kiss
So gagging on me must be your romantic definition of taking your breath away
Damn, is it a hoe's mentality
Or is it a whole mentally
That you realize in the end
we will both have one thing in common
So who's really being used
I learned that honesty gets you more cheeks
Than a grandma at a day care
But there's no kids in my room
Just lessons being taught
And females constantly ask me
Rodney
Why don't you write sex poetry
I say because I want to do more than just make you wet
Pussy aint nothing but a 5-letter word
Contorted into a woman's worth
But I want women to be more than leaky faucets
and late night soaked bedsheets
Trust
I'm not sexually discreet
Just saving what you seek for a better time at hand
But it seems as though your palms grasp all odds against you
So your values hold no redemption
All tension
That's probably why you only scratch x's into my back
Not listening
No o's
No feelings
Just condoms with more ambition

Than what I'm witnessing
No eyes watching
No vision
The mental aspect of a blind theme with one mission
Exploiting your body like a fresh murder
So yellow tape surpasses the crime scene
But physically giving
And speaking of giving's
That reminds me
You can pass the Trojan that I will gladly use
But I still find no complacency with a meaningless lifestyle

Complacence

Complacence
When did our people get complacent
With a life that's shapeless
Was it
Broken dreams from past prophets
Present hopelessness
Or is their minds and the "master's" plan adjacent
A psychological slaveship
If so
The streets need a shape shift
A face lift because these behaviors are getting old
Wrinkles in time
When you think everything that's good is really the sinner's role
Well I serve the true author
The chronological barber
When the edge ups and tapes lines continue to grow further from the truth
We come from rich bloodlines

Higher echelon
Etiquette
Compassion for life that can only be heaven sent
But when you look into society and try to find where the heavens went
It became lost in "fun" in the actions were effortless
Take a minute to let this settle in
Reflect
Are you helping the destruction or blessing it
To be socially elect vs a rebel for God
The benevolent against Satan's confederates
You choose
I just hope that the better wins
Cause in the end it's only your soul that's given
But this is not about religion
More about living
Rebelling against a system that's confiscating our wisdom
A criteria for suicidal symptoms
And I'm explaining their mission
Listen
These streets are a death wish
Youngins buying pairs to shoot
Lives are in a free fall
I'm trying to be the parachute
In my city
DC
You can get killed over jays
But they claim to God we sharing shoes
You see here's where our people lose
Because we were brought here to be lost
We/re selling ourselves short to the wrong cost
And for the wrong cause
Everything possible is being done
What happened to our leaders' sons
Our family trees are being smoked away, choked decayed, rolling to faze
And when it all fades
You're still stuck on the block with nothing to rebound from
When these actions continue

Life is like the turn tables and the resounds won
If you feel me
You will realize silent testimonies have no place in worldly struggles
I'm not prophet
I use logic
We all have lounges to birth topics
Why isn't this the gossip
Respect yourselves to expect some help
Let me ask you
Where do you want to be in the next 5 years
And if it's here
Then you achieved true happiness
But if it's not
Im probably sure it has something to do with fear
And fear is not a resolution
But a self-conflict to prevent a mental revolution
Yes, resist change
Resist facts
Yes, resist this random "nigga" speaking knowledge
Yes, resist operating your eyes the way God intended
Therefore, being blind is a misused diagnosis when the populous deny a sense
No, no, no
Free your mind body and soul
Easily said
Hard to achieve
But with this there would be no complacency to exist

Struggling Hearts

Our love
Our love it has never been perfect
But perfection is just a word inscribed into the minds
of those who refuse to settle
for the art gallery assembled in front of them
The scripture of eternity placed on a display case
Between the cavern we call our hearts
Our love created by selfish intentions
Routing the mind to receive sinful signals
Just to TiVo events we can do without
Adding
Adding more scars circumcised into our flesh
What tainted calligraphies we possess
But Every wrinkle formed on you is a blemish I want to erase from existence
Every suicidal thought you ever conceived will defuse
When you birth this life fixated in the panels of my vault

You are the robber that I would willingly deliver my profits to
Just to know your pain is deducted
Because Every withdrawal you take leaves me wanting more
My mission is to confiscate every negative thought you have about yourself
And break it down into a staircase that will forever be stepped on
Origami has no place in this relationship
Because only I can mold the peace of mind
That will piece together not the swan
But the lake that which she floats on
Every adolescent knew how to make the duck
But the lake
The lake I make will forever stay calm
because there are no rocks to be thrown
Rippling through your beauty just to skip a segment of their misusage
No logs protruding from within
Waiting for infidelity to seep through
There's only us dancing on the surface in triumph from past afflictions
Us following God's shadow manifesting what we call FUTURE

Religious Ball Game

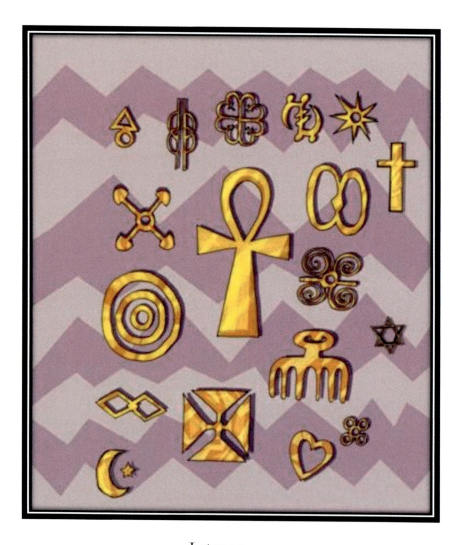

Let me guess
You think all Muslims are terrorist
You think that the Quran preaches suicidal bombings to get God's wings
Do you believe Christians promote school killings and crimes sprees
Naw but it happens though
You get your knowledge from media and action shows

The biggest racism to speak on any other position than what they call their own
They talk behind your backs too
But you believe their words so the hate's engraved seamed and grown
But why would they do the same to religion
The precision behind God's wisdom
Are you serious that's a key mission
The division in life's living
And you in Pinocchio's position
Listening to fraud schism
A puppets act
But they perfected lies and deceit
Because media created the hate
And left you pulling your own strings
Judging before you read any other scripture than what you call your own
The ignorance in mankind
When the Holy Torah, Bible and Quran are all blueprints in the Grand design
I was victim once too
Side tracked on who's the messenger but refusing to see the message
When each prophet submitted to Allah /God
And through them you saw his reflection
It's the correction to the blessings we seek for
When you're eating off the fruit but leaving the pieced core
My practice might be different from yours
His practice might be different than ours
But we all worship on the same court
The ball game is access into heaven and not hell
Eternal peace and not eternal jail
Where's the logic in living refraining from sin
And someone who believes different
Doesn't train
But has gained access in
Why would God place religion in a category of competition
Why would he want man to fight for his holy existence
When no one acknowledges Jews even though Jesus wasn't Christian

And no one knew about Muslims before the twin tower collusion
So know your facts
Fear is the only way the wrong people can profit
You let them control your optics
To be blind
Even though their hands are all in your pockets
So ask yourself do you have knowledge
Or do you believe America birth any Biblical Prophets

The Verdict

Oh how the intelligent have fallen
To be or not be a part of the script
Those who write their own destiny are scrutinized
By the eyes of their own brothers and sisters
Gaining freedom would be an easier task with group effort
Yet, You see
The people tell you
We are free
you are crazy

And why Are you acting out against the system
The system
Constantly playing them like old cartridges
Blowing away the bonds of our future and systemically cleaning the legacy left behind by our ancestors
That's a Nintendo reference for those who still think this is a game
We have watched our blood spill on this country for how many generations now
But they tell us we are crazy
Not knowing people like us are the only boundary delaying them from finishing the job
So I came early to the interview
With my own pay stub and a middle finger
Saying fuck you
We will not let you continue to take innocent lives
And imprison millions of minds
You see
Fiction is the nonfiction we live in
They could tell us we were rescued from Africa and still some would listen
That's why it's our mission
To break down stories, lies, and propaganda so your Third Eye can glisten
The vision
We must see fit that it's completed
Our ancestors did not give their lives so the elite could prosper
Our people have fallen distant from their roots
Social media has brainwashed you to do anything for attention
Trading wisdom for mentions
Men wearing clothes that don't fit them
Females allowing bitch to be the term used to get them
Who's going to listen
We are all gods and goddesses
Yet the police show us different
And not to generalize because sometimes
Sometimes they are the only ones standing between a shell and an innocent life
But tell me when is it ever right for them to have the criminal mind
They're supposed to uphold a code of conduct

But take no responsibility when wrong is committed
You have sworn to protect us
Yet you neglect us
Does our skin color hold no compassion for your laws
Does this melanin we embrace make you scared of your flaws
Because you are killing without probable cause
You see
This is the justice system we live in
And all we want is change, peace, and equality for our children
And our children's children to build a better connection
So please tell me how is this an unfair correction
Dear congress, dear government, dear mankind are you listening
Are you even trying anymore
Or is us being the minority your only objection

Are You an OG

Dear nigga
You know they want you dead right
You know every time you leave your stoup
Your block
They plotting to shoot you in the head right
Yeah man those blue and whites be reckless
You talking bout the Feds right

Naw I'm talking bout niggas just like you
Their bandana holds their threads tight
Dear nigga
You know they want you dead right
You know every time you make green
They're coming for your pockets
Those reds in office republicans be wildin
Wall street
Stock lifts
Taxes keep being raised
Naw I'm talking those with the burner
Bleeding
Trying to off us
With the heat that's being raised
No temperatures recorded
Because it's ironic their insides are frozen
I guess that's how their emotions
Evens out between the tool and the man
I wonder are they even man
Lost souls
Wandering the fields refraining from picking cotton
Instead taking out their family trees
You're not even niggas
You're Africans brought here
Now enslaved by ignorance
bliss
Is forbidden
Now living to wish
Change
Because the old heads said it was going to come
Some day
When
I don't know
I could've sworn rights were given
Now the generations are shifting on their own
Who's to blame
When did gaining knowledge become lame
When did gutter balls in life become the main lane
Satisfying the outlook bowling for self strain

Only this one's internal
When you look in a mirrors frame
Does your reflection stare the same way you feel
If not, it's time to change
So to the gangs
You were created to help the community
Explain what happened OG
When did your creed go wrong
Was it when the ones in the background
That's leading the traps now
Were inducted without having their backgrounds checked
I can't say
Just know your history
Support your foundation's positivity to build your rep and gain a name
Instead of taking lives meaningless with the set you claim

Casket Coated Mindset

"I grew up I was a screw up been introduced to the game and now I Fucking blew up"
But now I wish to screw down
Biggie was an inspiration
But I don't want to die with that lifestyle
I want my eulogy to read
I was good man

While leaving a notorious legacy
No scarface carbon copy
No mansion
No drugs under my belt
There's no Italian in my bloodline
Yet Al Pacino moves my race more than Malcolm X, Martin Luther King, and Nelson Mandela
That's a sad thought
To not know yourself
Without your history
A positive future can't be embraced
Yet you remain a slave
It's a constant competition amongst the blind
Eyes wide open
Without their pupils catching the concept
Don't take this out of context
I was once a visionary amongst sheep
All inducive yet little facts in my speech
Now every word my lips birth are conclusive
Fully awoken no
I don't believe so
But if knowledge was currency
I wouldn't want to take blame for making change
If I can't help others make change
Because I wish to break banks
So currently I'm in the process
Of floating my people from a casket coated mindset
That dollar signs can't keep your pockets full when you die

The Contract

What is your soul destined for
A subscription that holds self-depiction on contact
Rarely talked about but often done
My pen holds true to Gods work
Like his Devine son.
Yes, the famous one
No, no, no
The famous won
Because fame equals evils name

But most perceive them as saviors and idolize the majors
Not realizing they have signed the dotted line of Satan
The truth is surfaced but the blind calls it hating
When will your eyes be awakened

The Final Rest

Energy is immortal
One's life cannot be comprised of the time spent in flesh
Do not fear the inevitable
Death is a part of the Creator's contract
Just as birth is
And on Wednesday June 24th Thomas Edward Hart Jr complied
with his agreement
A guardian
Turned ancestor that will always be remembered

No longer burdened by his physical suffering
He exists where existence is infinite
Take your time to contemplate his legacy and the beautiful family
that
he has left behind
Carry his smile intact
Strong and bold
Brave and wise
The courage not to mourn for your lost but to rejoice for his spirit
The transformation is truly a beautiful one
This bittersweet thing we call life
It is the greatest blessing anyone can grant
But it is also this paradigms final rest

Death's Wish

Death's Wish Scattered deception
An abyss destined heart turned evil for a Job
Am I forced to be this way
To make a living off of others souls
Or am I intrigued by it
Do I like my occupation
While I'm consuming a man's last breath on this sinned infested planet
Or am I trying to set them free from constant suffering
Where does my immortal essence reside
As I commit my number
Infinite homicide
I burst into tears
I ask God

Why am I the only one to bare this immense burden
A burden that I carry bottled up not like a love note
But like suicidal suns willing to disperse
Just to end any and every affliction in their universe
I refuse to let my tribulations continue
Handing over my scythe
Let it be known that DEATH quits

The Rehearsal

The blind speak smooth
because they will never see the light of day
No visual memories from the past, present, or future
I wonder when they dream do they see internal heartbeats attached to
a silicone soul
A constant hallucination
Or is it the divine truth
The skill to say I see right through you
Without capturing the outline of an innocent demon
occupying flesh
I too possess a gift from Allah
Déjà vu
The strength of the Nile
The passion to see premonitions before they happen

but I can't reverse the actions to save my life
So is this really a curse
To know a situation will become worse
but you don't sketch out the actors from a scene even though in your mind it's rehearsed
Dreams that are habitual lies
They're committed to indulge your fantasies
Then in a split second you're born again to the horror show called reality
A nightmare doesn't seem so bad when your life contains monsters
When your thought process can't even trust itself to resist death
When populous around you is oblivious of what to expect
When the struggle Is the only thing persistent in life
I would rather be committed to rest

When Will We

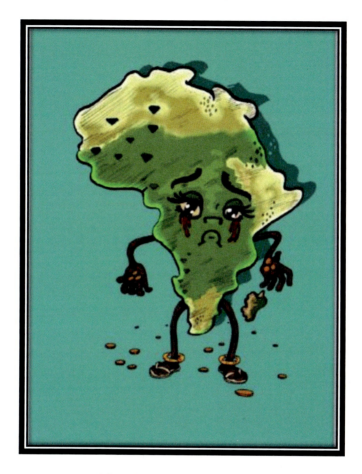

They know where you live
They know where you sleep
Since birth you have been tracked down with a number encoded
Is it revelations decoded
The government says it in the people's best interest
and we let them take over
Is it The New World Order
Lives reordered for the frame of mind
Intertwined with echoes of lost souls
The NSA spies on you
So when you act out
They will be listening

Will you let them prevail
The matrix is real
Really real
Too bad our life has no Neo living along side of us for hope
They say that "Jesus is destined to come back"
Why the fuck are we waiting on a savior for
I'm trying to rebuild a heaven on earth now
So when he does show up
He can commend us for doing more than just wearing his symbol of death
Is there any freedom left
When will too late be decided
Shotgun buck in your face at your front door
This came to me in a revelation like form in a span of 5 mins
Does that make a prophet
or I'm I just a man trying to help
Willing to digest the process
How can the heavens respect us when we can't even take control of our own lives
Stop believing in the world's lies
When will we stop hitting the snooze alarm
Get out of this brainwashed mentality
We see the wrong being done and we say nothing
We do nothing
When did we drop our guard down
When did we let this hippie look alike become our God now
When will we stop letting them rape mother Africa
When will we remember everything about us
because our actions seem clandestine
When will we stop complaining
When will we WAKE UP

Mothers Reflection

Before I could tic my own shoes
you were my security
laced up for all my battles
A Warrior and a Goddess molted down into flesh
Childhood without you
would have been equivalent to the death penalty

Because any female above a certain age can give birth
to a seed
But it takes a woman
with a tree trunk mentality to raise maturity
And God knows you endured forest fires
So we all need our mothers.
A lover, a protector, and a swift punisher when we step out of line
Because rebellious nature would cease to continue
with a foot up my asphalt
The ground you constantly picked me up from
and steered me away from repeat
You taught me about the nightmares of life
The effort you must put in to sleep peacefully
Even when times I thought to be inadequate you helped me defeat
thee
As your son we share more than just resemblance
I just hope that this partial reflection of yours
can live up to your legacy
You bared the burden of me for 9 months
It's time that I return the favor and carry you for a lifetime

The Closure

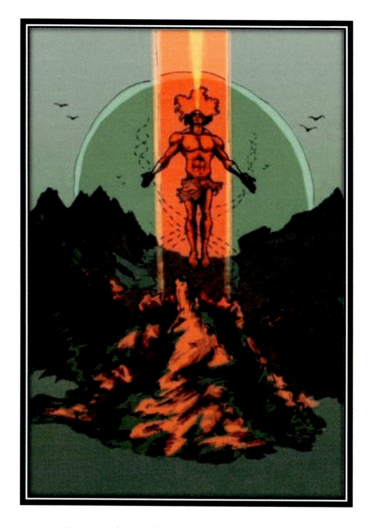

I was reborn the day I picked up a pen
Ever since my pages ran thin
A seed was planted
My mind expanded and "The Initiation" was complete
I was blessed with a dream
A vision
That I would nurse until death
Growing up with less melanin than my peers

I wondered
What could I produce to fixate someone's veins of darker complexion
Later I realized
We are all "struggling hearts" trying to find existence in a plane
Where the mind has been taught that everything which makes you human is false
And that God is a reflection of a "Religious Ball Game" between covenants of different faiths
No
God is in a new born baby's face
God is in nature
God is in the stars
God is in "A Mothers Reflection"
Which means God is in you
They have established rules on "How to Tame a Sinner"
"When Will We" realize we must "Unlearn" this "Negative Immune System"
Realize that love is all we need
It is either prosper in connection or die divided
You hold the key
I hope that you are listening as I preach
"The Contract" has been breached by those who have been placed into power
"Complacence" has played us for fatal attraction
It is the age of information
There is no excuse
Yet most live for writing "Letters to the Weeknd" and "Letters to the Jump Offs"
Doing anything for pleasure
Granting "Death's Wish" with the slogan
The sooner the better
Only to find a "Beautiful Deception" with every endeavor
"Stand" up for what you believe in
You will not be alone
I will be on the frontline with those not practicing "The Rehearsal" of humanity
Granting more than a "Casket Coated Mindset"
Classism has no distinction here

"The Verdict" will "Find You First"
That may be positive for some and negative for others
Are you a doctor
a lawyer
a thinker
Are you on the street corner
"Are you an OG"
Are you someone who wants to see this world rise together
Every single breath taken is one step closer to "The Final Rest"
We must all unite
Me, you, men, women, and children of every race
So that "God's Plan for a shaded Revolution" can take place

Made in the USA
Columbia, SC
05 October 2018